SCHOLASTIC

CLOSE READING

FICTION

AGES 10+

Scholastic Education, an imprint of Scholastic Ltd
Book End, Range Road, Witney, Oxfordshire, OX29 0YD
Registered office: Westfield Road, Southam, Warwickshire CV47 0RA
www.scholastic.co.uk
© 2016, Scholastic Inc. © 2019, Scholastic Ltd
1 2 3 4 5 6 7 8 9   9 0 1 2 3 4 5 6 7 8

British Library Cataloguing-in-Publication Data
A catalogue record for this book is available from the British Library.
ISBN 978-1407-18279-7

Printed and bound by Ashford Colour Press

Author
Marcia Miller, Martin Lee
Editorial
Rachel Morgan, Louise Titley, Jane Wood and Rebecca Rothwell
Cover and Series Design
Scholastic Design Team: Nicolle Thomas, Neil Salt and Alice Duggan
Illustrations
Doug Jones, Kelly Kennedy, Michael Moran, Jason Robinson and Gemma Hastilow

UK Revised Edition. Originally published by Scholastic Inc, 557 Broadway, New York, NY 10012 (ISBN: 978-0-545-79388-9)

Contents

| Texts and Questions |

Character

Point of View

Setting/Mood

Key Events & Details

Sequence of Events

Conflict & Resolution

Context Clues

Compare & Contrast

Make Inferences

Summarise

Introduction

Texts For Close Reading and Deep Comprehension

Close reading involves careful study of a short text passage to build a deep, critical understanding of the text. By developing children's comprehension and higher-order thinking skills, you can help them make sense of the world.

> "A significant body of research links the close reading of complex text – whether the student is a struggling reader or advanced – to significant gains in reading proficiency, and finds close reading to be a key component of college and career readiness."
> (Partnership for Assessment of Readiness for College and Careers, 2012, p7)

Reading and Re-Reading For Different Purposes

The texts in *Close Reading* are carefully selected and deliberately short. This focuses children on purposeful reading, re-reading and responding. They learn about the topic through rich vocabulary development and deep comprehension.

Children re-read and analyse the text through questioning to explore:

- text structure and features
- key ideas and details
- connections/conclusions
- predictions/inferences
- words and phrases in context.

Children actively respond to the text using:

- higher-order thinking skills
- paired discussion
- written responses.

Text Marking: A Powerful Active-Reading Strategy

To improve their comprehension of literary texts, children must actively engage with the material. Careful and consistent text marking by hand is one valuable way to accomplish this. The true goal of teaching text marking is to help children internalise an effective close-reading strategy, not to have them show how many marks they can make on a page. Text-marking skills are encouraged in each passage.

Introduction

About the Texts and Questions

This book provides 20 reproducible texts that address ten key reading-comprehension skills:

- Character
- Point of View
- Setting/Mood
- Key Events & Details
- Sequence of Events
- Conflict & Resolution
- Context Clues
- Compare & Contrast
- Make Inferences
- Summarise

The contents pages detail the skills and genres covered as well as the Lexile score (see page 7). The passages are stand-alone texts that can be used in any order you choose by individuals, pairs, groups or the whole class. (See page 9 for a close-reading routine to model.)

Following each passage is a reproducible 'Questions' page of text-dependent comprehension questions.

Answers are provided. They include sample text marking and answers. Encourage children to self-assess and revise their answers as you review the text markings together. This approach encourages discussion, comparison, extension, reinforcement and correlation to other reading skills.

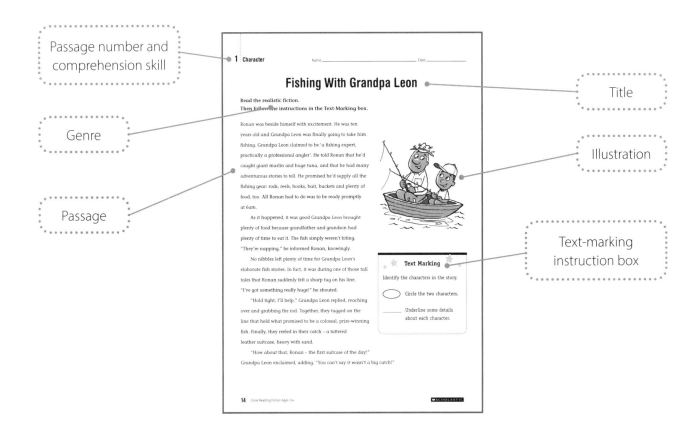

Passage number and comprehension skill

Genre

Passage

Title

Illustration

Text-marking instruction box

SCHOLASTIC

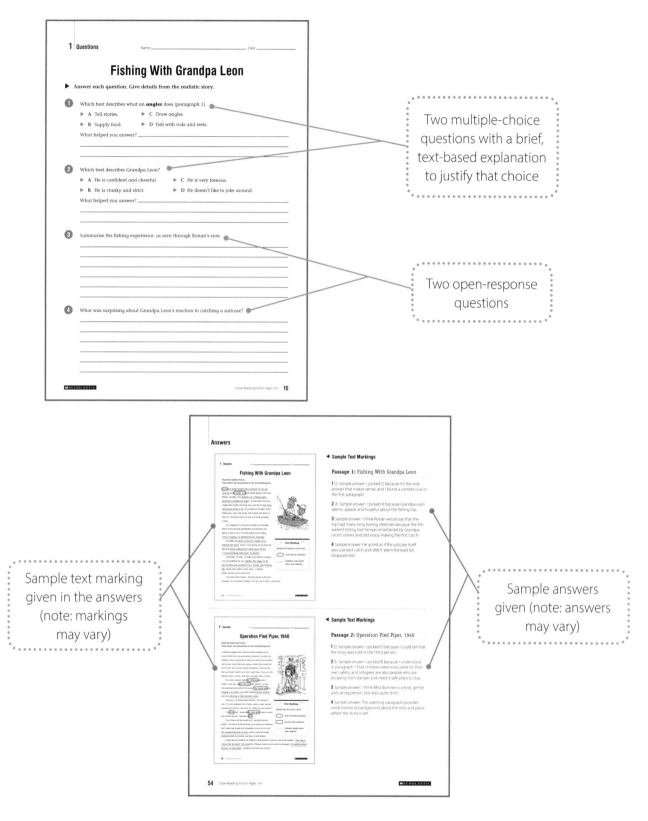

Two multiple-choice questions with a brief, text-based explanation to justify that choice

Two open-response questions

Sample text marking given in the answers (note: markings may vary)

Sample answers given (note: answers may vary)

Lexiles

The Lexile Framework® finds the right books for children by measuring readers and texts on the same scale. Lexile measures are the global standard in reading assessment and are accurate for all ages, including first- and second-language learners. The Lexile scores fall within the ranges recommended for children aged 10+. (The poem on page 46 does not include a Lexile score because poetry is excluded from Lexile measurements.)

Introduction

Comprehension Skill Summary Cards

Comprehension Skill Summary Cards are provided on pages 11–13 to help support the children. The terms in bold are the same ones the children will identify as they mark the text.

Give children the relevant card before providing them with the text passage. Discuss the skill together to ensure that children understand it. Encourage the children to use the cards as a set of reading aids to refer to whenever they read any type of fiction text or display the cards in your classroom.

Comprehension Skill
Character

Characters take part in the events of the story. A character can be a person, an animal or a thing.

- Read for details that describe each character.
- Notice differences among characters so you can tell them apart.
- Notice whether and how a character changes or learns during the story.

A story may have a **main character** and one or more **minor characters**.

- The main character is the most important character in the story.
- A minor character is not the focus of the story.

Comprehension Skill
Key Events & Details

Events are the actions or things that happen in a story. The events build interest and move the story along. But not all events have the same effect on the story.

As you read, think about which actions or things are **key events** and which are **details**.

- A key event is important to the theme or big idea of the story.
- Details tell more about a key event. Details may answer questions, such as *Who? Where? What? When? Why?* or *How?*

Comprehension Skill
Point of View

Knowing *who* is telling a story gives you its **point of view**. What you learn in the story comes through that point of view. Authors usually use one of two points of view.

First-person point of view has a character *in* the story telling it. In first-person stories, readers learn about events from that character's point of view. Look for words like *I, me* and *we*.

Third-person point of view has someone *outside* the story telling it. That person is the **narrator**. In third-person stories, readers learn the thoughts, actions and feelings of many characters. Look for words like *he, she* and *they*.

Tips and Suggestions

- The text-marking process is adaptable. While numbering, boxing, circling and underlining are the most common methods, you can personalise the strategy for your class. You might ask the children to use letters to mark text; for example, write 'MC' to indicate a main character, 'D' to mark a detail, or '1st' for first person and '3rd' for third person. Whichever technique you use, focus on the need for consistency of marking.

- You may wish to extend the text-marking strategy by asking the children to identify other aspects of writing, such as confusing words, expressions or idioms. You can also encourage them to write their own notes and questions in the margins.

SCHOLASTIC

Teaching Routine for Close Reading and Text Marking

Here is one suggested routine to use Close Reading and Text Marking in the classroom.

Preview

- **Engage prior knowledge** of the passage topic and its genre. Help children link it to similar topics or examples of the genre they may have read.

- **Identify the reading skill** for which children will be marking the text. Display or distribute the relevant Comprehension Skill Summary Card and review these together. (See Comprehension Skill Summary Cards, page 8.)

Model *(for the first passage, to familiarise children with the process)*

- **Display the passage** and provide children with their own copy. Look at the text together by reading the title and looking at the illustration.

- **Draw attention to the markings** children will use to enhance their understanding of the passage. Link the text-marking box to the Comprehension Skill Summary Card for clarification.

- **Read aloud the passage** as children follow along. Guide children to think about the featured skill and to note any questions they may have on sticky notes.

- **Mark the text together.** Begin by numbering the paragraphs. Then discuss the choices you make when marking the text, demonstrating and explaining how various text elements support the skill. Check that children understand how to mark the text using the icons and graphics shown in the text-marking box.

Read

- **Display each passage for a shared reading experience.** Do a quick read of the passage together to familiarise the children with it. Then read it together a second time, pausing as necessary to answer questions, draw connections or clarify words as needed. Then read the passage once more, this time with an eye to the text features described in the text-marking box.

- **Invite children to offer ideas for additional markings.** These might include noting unfamiliar vocabulary, an idiom or phrase they may not understand, or an especially interesting, unusual, or important detail they want to remember. Model how to use sticky notes, coloured pencils, highlighters or question marks.

Respond

- **Ask the children to read the passage independently.** This fourth reading is intended to allow the children to mark the text themselves. It will also prepare them to discuss the piece and offer their views about it.

- **Ask the children to answer the questions on the companion questions page.** Encourage them to look back at their text markings and other text evidence. This will help the children to provide complete and supported responses.

National Curriculum Correlation

	Passages
• continuing to read and discuss an increasingly wide range of fiction	1–20
• identifying and discussing themes and conventions in and across a wide range of writing	3, 11, 13, 14, 15, 18
• making comparisons within books	15, 16, 18
• checking that the book makes sense to them, discussing their understanding and exploring the meaning of words in context	2, 3, 4, 5, 7, 8, 11, 13, 14, 15, 16, 20
• drawing inferences such as inferring characters' feelings, thoughts and motives from their actions, and justifying inferences with evidence	1–20
• predicting what might happen from details stated and implied	4
• summarising the main ideas drawn from more than one paragraph, identifying key details that support the main ideas	1, 5, 7, 8, 10, 15, 19, 20
• identifying how language, structure and presentation contribute to meaning	2, 7, 13, 14, 17
• discuss and evaluate how authors use language, including figurative language, considering the impact on the reader	3, 9, 17

■SCHOLASTIC

Character

Characters take part in the events of the story. A character can be a person, an animal or a thing.

- Read for details that describe each character.
- Notice differences among characters so you can tell them apart.
- Notice whether and how a character changes or learns during the story.

A story may have a **main character** and one or more **minor characters**.

- The main character is the most important character in the story.
- A minor character is not the focus of the story.

Point of View

Knowing *who* is telling a story gives you its **point of view**. What you learn in the story comes through that point of view. Authors usually use one of two points of view.

- **First-person** point of view has a character *in* the story telling it. In first-person stories, readers learn about events from that character's point of view. Look for words like *I*, *me* and *we*.
- **Third-person** point of view has someone *outside* the story telling it. That person is the **narrator**. In third-person stories, readers learn the thoughts, actions and feelings of many characters. Look for words like *he*, *she* and *they*.

Setting/Mood

The **setting** of a story tells *where* and *when* the story takes place. The setting can help create the **mood** or feeling of the story.

Read for details that tell where a story takes place.

- It can be a *real* place.
- It can be an *imaginary* place.

Read for details that tell when a story takes place.

- It might be set in the *present* (now).
- It might be set in the *past* (long ago).
- It might be set in the *future* (years from now).

Key Events & Details

Events are the actions or things that happen in a story. The events build interest and move the story along. But not all events have the same effect on the story.

As you read, think about which actions or things are **key events** and which are **details**.

- A key event is important to the theme or big idea of the story.
- Details tell more about a key event. Details may answer questions, such as *Who? Where? What? When? Why?* or *How?*

Sequence of Events

In most stories, events happen in a certain order or **sequence**. Some events happen in the *beginning* of the story. Other things happen in the *middle*. The story finishes with events that happen at the *end*.

- As you read, think about the sequence of events. This helps you follow the story. Picture the events in your mind to help you remember the sequence.
- **Signal words** give clues about the sequence of events. (Examples: *before, first, second, next, then, now, later, after* and *finally*; as well as specific dates and times.)

Conflict & Resolution

Good stories have a **plot**. The plot is the set of key events that move the story along. Most stories present a problem and how it gets solved. This relationship is called **conflict and resolution**.

- A conflict is a form of trouble, problem or disagreement.
- A resolution is the way the conflict gets solved.
- **Signal words** are clues to a conflict and its resolution. (Examples for conflicts: *question, challenge, dilemma, puzzle, need* and *trouble*. Examples for resolutions: *answer, result, idea, plan, reason, solution, solve, improve* and *fix*.)

Context Clues

Authors may use words you may not know. But nearby words or sentences can offer clues about the meaning of an unknown word.

- **Context** refers to all the words and sentences around an unknown word.
- **Context clues** are hints that can help you work out a word's meaning. As you read, search for related words, such as synonyms, antonyms, explanations or examples in nearby text. Link these clues to the unknown word to understand it.

Compare & Contrast

Authors often discuss people, places, things or ideas by describing how they are alike and ways they differ.

- To **compare** means to tell how two or more things are alike.
- To **contrast** means to tell how two or more things are different.
- Comparing and contrasting help you understand a story's ideas, its plot, its characters and its message.
- **Signal words** give clues that help you compare and contrast. (Examples for comparing: *both, too, like, also* and *in the same way*. Examples for contrasting: *but, only, however, unlike* and *different*.)

Make Inferences

Authors may hint at an idea without stating it directly. But they usually include enough detail so readers can use what they already know about a topic to 'read between the lines' and work out a hidden message.

- **Text clues** are words or details that help you work out an unstated idea.

- You **make an inference** by combining text clues with what you already know to form a likely conclusion or 'educated guess'.

Summarise

As you read, check that you understand and can recall the key elements of a story. Think about how to retell the important parts in your own words. Leave out minor details and get to the point.

- The **topic** or **theme** of a story is its focus – what it is mainly about.

- **Key details** add more information and support the story's theme.

- A **summary** briefly restates the theme using only the key details. A good summary is short, clear and tells only what is most important.

Name _____ Date _____

Fishing With Grandpa Leon

Read the realistic fiction.
Then follow the instructions in the Text-Marking box.

Ronan was beside himself with excitement. He was ten years old and Grandpa Leon was finally going to take him fishing. Grandpa Leon claimed to be 'a fishing expert, practically a professional angler'. He told Ronan that he'd caught giant marlin and huge tuna, and that he had many adventurous stories to tell. He promised he'd supply all the fishing gear: rods, reels, hooks, bait, buckets and plenty of food, too. All Ronan had to do was to be ready promptly at 6am.

As it happened, it was good Grandpa Leon brought plenty of food because grandfather and grandson had plenty of time to eat it. The fish simply weren't biting. "They're napping," he informed Ronan, knowingly.

No nibbles left plenty of time for Grandpa Leon's elaborate fish stories. In fact, it was during one of those tall tales that Ronan suddenly felt a sharp tug on his line. "I've got something really huge!" he shouted.

"Hold tight, I'll help," Grandpa Leon replied, reaching over and grabbing the rod. Together, they tugged on the line that held what promised to be a colossal, prize-winning fish. Finally, they reeled in their catch – a tattered leather suitcase, heavy with sand.

"How about that, Ronan – the first suitcase of the day!" Grandpa Leon exclaimed, adding, "You can't say it wasn't a big catch!"

Text Marking

Identify the characters in the story.

⬭ Circle the two characters.

_____ Underline some details about each character.

Name _____ Date _____

Fishing With Grandpa Leon

▶ **Answer each question. Give details from the realistic story.**

1 Which best describes what an **angler** does (paragraph 1).

▶ **A** Tell stories.　　▶ **C** Draw angles.

▶ **B** Supply food.　　▶ **D** Fish with rods and reels.

What helped you answer? _____

_____

_____

2 Which best describes Grandpa Leon?

▶ **A** He is confident and cheerful.　　▶ **C** He is very famous.

▶ **B** He is cranky and strict.　　▶ **D** He doesn't like to joke around.

What helped you answer? _____

_____

_____

3 Summarise the fishing experience, as seen through Ronan's eyes.

_____

_____

_____

_____

_____

_____

4 What was surprising about Grandpa Leon's reaction to catching a suitcase?

_____

_____

_____

_____

_____

_____

Name _____ Date _____

Operation Pied Piper, 1940

Read the historical fiction.
Then follow the instructions in the Text-Marking box.

As Britain's biggest cities suffered enemy bombing in the Second World War, the government decided to evacuate city children to the countryside for their own safety. Most children had no idea where they were going or whom they would live with. When they arrived at their destination, carrying only their gas mask, identity card and a small bag, it was up to the billeting officer to find a host who could give them a home.

One rainy autumn night, Mr Wilkinson knocked briskly at the door of Miss Burrows. She opened it to find him standing there with two evacuees. The smaller girl was clinging to her sister's coat. Both looked tired and anxious, and were shivering in their drenched clothes.

"Dear me!" exclaimed Miss Burrows. "Two drowned rats, if I'm not mistaken! You'd better come in, girls, and dry yourselves by the fire," she went on. "What are your names?"

"I'm Vera, Miss," answered the older girl, trying to sound braver than she felt. "And this is Eve."

"You'd better call me Auntie Joy," said Miss Burrows, gently. "I'm sure we'll all get along if you mind your manners, don't make any trouble and remember to do as you're told." She sounded both kind yet stern, and Eve eyed her warily, wishing heartily her mother was there to hide behind.

Text Marking

Identify who the story is about.

⬭   Circle the adult characters.

▭   Box the child characters.

____   Underline details about each character.

Closing the door behind Mr Wilkinson, Miss Burrows turned to look at the children. "How long is it since their last meal?" she wondered. Whiskers trotted over to meet the strangers. Eve timidly stroked the furry cat and smiled – possibly for the first time all day.

Operation Pied Piper, 1940

▶ **Answer each question. Give details from the historical fiction.**

1 Who is telling this story?

▶ **A** Vera   ▶ **B** Eve   ▶ **C** Mr Wilkinson   ▶ **D** the narrator

What helped you answer? _____

_____

_____

2 Which is a synonym for **evacuees**?

▶ **A** strangers   ▶ **B** refugees   ▶ **C** enemies   ▶ **D** hosts

What helped you answer? _____

_____

_____

3 Make inferences using details from the story. What kind of person is Miss Burrows?

_____

_____

_____

_____

_____

_____

_____

_____

4 What is the purpose of the opening paragraph?

_____

_____

_____

_____

_____

_____

_____

The Expedition

Read the adventure story.
Then follow the instructions in the Text-Marking box.

They'd been trapped by ice for 36 days and had been on their own for longer than that, ever since a storm separated them from the ship and the rest of the crew on their expedition. Karl was in a pitiful state – lost, weak, frightened and shivering from unrelenting cold. He was also suffering the painful effects of frostbite.

Suddenly, ice cracked enough for the boat to break loose and begin to bob gently in the frigid sea. The crew cheered their good fortune. No longer stuck in the ice, their chances of survival had edged up a notch. But Karl understood that the struggles had not ended, as medical supplies were nearly gone and there was barely any food left. If that weren't terrifying enough, the maps were lost, too.

The crew navigated icy waters until their hands bled and muscles ached. For days, Karl saw nothing in the muted, constant light but other ice floes. Then, finally, he detected a sound in the stillness that he hadn't heard for months: the cawing of birds. That sweet sound signalled that land was near. All were exhilarated!

The land they found was snow-covered and flat. The crew rowed along its barren coast until they spotted the mouth of a river. Karl and the men entered, presuming it would lead to a village and safety. On they plodded, ever more hopeful of survival.

Text Marking

Identify who is telling this story.

☐ Box signal words that suggest who tells the story.

✗ Cross a box to show how the story is told.

☐ first person

☐ third person

_____ Underline words or phrases that tell about Karl.

The Expedition

▶ **Answer each question. Give details from the story.**

1 Which best states the theme of this story?

▶ **A** Boating   ▶ **B** Nature   ▶ **C** Survival   ▶ **D** Weather

What helped you answer? _____

_____

_____

2 Which word can replace **unrelenting** in the first paragraph without changing its meaning (paragraph 1)?

▶ **A** constant   ▶ **B** freezing   ▶ **C** pitiful   ▶ **D** terrifying

What helped you answer? _____

_____

_____

3 In paragraph 2, the narrator says '…their chances of survival had edged up a notch'. Why was the narrator not more enthusiastic at the moment?

_____

_____

_____

_____

_____

_____

4 Based on the details of this story, describe where you think it takes place.

_____

_____

_____

_____

_____

_____

The Record Setter

Read the humorous story.
Then follow the instructions in the Text-Marking box.

My brother, Alex, is generally considered to be a reliable, clever, thoughtful fellow. I say 'generally' because of things like what he's doing right now.

Picture this and you'll understand. While I, Nate, sit here playing a video game and texting with half my friends – two perfectly normal things to be doing for amusement – what is he occupied with? Alex is standing over there, counting softly to himself *79, 80, 81, 82...* while he repeatedly bats a rubber ball attached by an elastic string to a wooden paddle. This is nonsensical behaviour, is it not?

You might think I'm being too hard on Alex, as brothers sometimes can be to one another. On the contrary, I'm being lenient. You see, this time it's paddle-ball batting, but the last time – and I refer to just a few weeks ago – the challenge was standing on his head for as long as he could, with a timer set up on the rug. Of course, he had to read it upside down, but I suppose he got better at it day by day. Maybe he should've put the timer upside down, too.

Frankly, I'm getting a bit concerned. What if one of his weird pals introduces him to alligator wrestling? Or what if he gets enticed to take up tightrope walking from skyscraper to skyscraper? I tell you, for Alex, these ideas are not too far-fetched!

Text Marking

Identify the main character in this story. Read for clues about point of view.

☐ Box signal words that suggest who tells the story.

✗ Cross a box to show how the story is told.

☐ first person

☐ third person

◯ Circle the name of the main character.

_____ Underline words or phrases that describe the main character.

Name _____ Date _____

The Record Setter

▶ **Answer each question. Give details from the humorous story.**

1 To amuse himself, Nate likes to…

▶ **A** wrestle alligators.　　▶ **C** play table tennis.

▶ **B** praise his brother.　　▶ **D** play video games.

What helped you answer? _____

_____

_____

2 Which is a synonym for **lenient** (paragraph 3)?

▶ **A** easygoing　　▶ **B** critical　　▶ **C** loving　　▶ **D** harsh

What helped you answer? _____

_____

_____

3 How does Nate use exaggeration to get across his point about his brother's behaviour?

_____

_____

_____

_____

_____

_____

4 Imagine Alex describing Nate. How might the story be different?

_____

_____

_____

_____

_____

_____

The Beach House

Read the suspense story.
Then follow the instructions in the Text-Marking box.

The water was glistening in the summer's morning sunlight and the surf was cool on their feet as Krin and Paula happily strolled along the water's edge. Collecting shells and skimming stones as they went, the brother and sister were enjoying exploring what appeared to be a never-ending beach.

After a while, they stopped and looked back. Their parents and the umbrellas, chairs and crowds were a long way off. But just ahead, nestled among some trees, stood a run-down house. It appeared to be unoccupied; curious, they went to investigate.

The steps creaked as they ascended them, as did the porch when they stepped onto it. The shutters and porch railing were weathered and broken. The front door was ajar so they squeezed through and cautiously entered. The place was in total disarray, chock-a-block with dust, sand, dead leaves and overturned, splintered furniture. They'd taken but a few steps when the door unexpectedly slammed shut behind them.

Startled, Krin and Paula spun around. Before they could even utter something like "Uh-oh", the window shutters clapped closed, too. And if this wasn't scary enough, the stairs to the second floor squeaked. When a light in the back bedroom flickered, that was absolutely the final straw.

"Let's get out of here, Paula!" And out they ran, all the way back to those wonderful umbrellas, beach chairs and crowds.

Text Marking

Think about the setting and mood of the story.

☐ Box WHEN it takes place.

✗ Cross a box to show WHEN the story is set.

☐ past

☐ present

☐ future

⬭ Circle WHERE it takes place.

___ Underline details that set the mood.

Name _____ Date _____

The Beach House

▶ **Answer each question. Give details from the suspense story.**

1 Who is telling the story?

▶ **A** Krin   ▶ **B** Paula   ▶ **C** a narrator   ▶ **D** a ghost

What helped you answer? _____

_____

_____

2 Things that are **chock-a-block** (paragraph 3) are _____.

▶ **A** full of blocks   ▶ **B** crowded together   ▶ **C** run-down   ▶ **D** broken

What helped you answer? _____

_____

_____

3 Why did Krin and Paula end up viewing the crowded beach as **wonderful** (paragraph 5)?

_____

_____

_____

_____

_____

_____

4 Summarise the setting and moods of the story. How does the mood change?

_____

_____

_____

_____

_____

_____

_____

_____

Name _____ Date _____

Mile-and-a-Quarter Monkey

Read the descriptive story.
Then follow the instructions in the Text-Marking box.

It had taken us nearly five hours from the river to reach Three-Mile House that hot summer day in the Grand Canyon. We were already tiring from the hike, and knowing that a relentlessly uphill slog still lay ahead, we gratefully rested there.

The path wound upwards through awesome – in the true sense of the word – scenery, rich with spectacular rock formations. The other hikers in the hut, also fatigued from their challenging climbs, seemed in an upbeat mood. Eventually, we gathered our courage to resume the twisting path to the rim.

Mile-and-a-Half House was our next stopping point, and reaching it was a steady struggle. Our muscles ached, our gusto was diminished and we were drained upon arrival. After a much-appreciated second rest, longer than our first, we reluctantly began the final leg of our ascent.

The hike was not getting any easier in the heat, and we paused continuously. While wishing the trek were over, we spotted it overhead: an immense monkey face! That's precisely what the eroded rocks looked like. We excitedly told everyone we passed about where to see Mile-and-a-Quarter Monkey, as we named it. Each hiker gladly promised to keep a lookout for it. Suddenly, amazingly, we felt a renewed bounce in our step. Discovering the giant monkey face had put wings on our feet. Energised, we practically flew out of the canyon, and that was awesome, too.

Text Marking

Think about the setting and mood of the story.

☐ Box WHEN it takes place.

⬭ Circle WHERE it takes place.

✗ Cross a box to show the setting.

   ☐ realistic

   ☐ imaginary

_____ Underline details that set the mood.

Mile-and-a-Quarter Monkey

▶ **Answer each question. Give details from the story.**

1 What best describes the mood of the hikers as they approached their second rest stop?

▶ **A** bored and miserable   ▶ **C** exhausted and a little grumpy

▶ **B** gloomy and disappointed   ▶ **D** cheerful and full of anticipation

What helped you answer? _____

_____

_____

2 Which would be a **trek** (paragraph 4)?

▶ **A** a car ride to the shops   ▶ **C** a skateboard ride down a hill

▶ **B** a lengthy hike in the snow   ▶ **D** a relaxing stroll around the block

What helped you answer? _____

_____

_____

3 What factors made the hike so challenging?

_____

_____

_____

_____

_____

_____

4 Explain the reason for the hikers' change in mood on the final leg of their ascent.

_____

_____

_____

_____

_____

_____

Medieval Festival

Read the fantasy.
Then follow the instructions in the Text-Marking box.

Driving to the Medieval Festival, Mum sang old folksongs while Gavin studied the long list of events. There would be sword classes, blacksmithing, acrobats, dancers, jesters and more, but it was jousting that was his top priority.

When the two entered the festival grounds, a whirl of sights, sounds and smells overwhelmed them. Sheep and goats grazed beside horses and mules. The scent of mead perfumed the air while strolling jugglers and musicians entertained the crowds. As Gavin pulled Mum towards the jousting field, he was so busy gawking that he tripped and fell. When he arose, his mother was gone and his body felt unusually heavy. Yikes! He was wearing a full suit of armour!

"Sir, your steed awaits!" announced a man in a cloak, directing Gavin towards the stable. Too stunned to protest, Gavin clanked along, huffing under the armour's weight.

> ## Text Marking
>
> Think about the key events in Gavin's experience.
>
>   Circle at least three key events.
>
> _____   Underline details about each event.

"I think you're mistaken," Gavin sputtered.

"Not so!" replied the squire. "Queen Mab commands you to replace Sir Harry, who broke his arm yesterday. Ride proudly to honour her!"

Gavin gulped, feeling equally confused and thrilled at this crazy turn of events. He'd wanted to see a joust, but to actually participate in one? Wow!

The squire paraded Gavin and his horse into position and handed him the long pole. Across the field was his fierce opponent, fully armoured and ready…

Medieval Festival

▶ **Answer each question. Give details from the fantasy.**

1 What is the main purpose of a Medieval Festival?

▶ **A** It is a great place to drink mead.

▶ **B** It allows visitors to see farm animals up close.

▶ **C** It lets people experience medieval events and activities.

▶ **D** It provides a chance for people to practise battle skills.

What helped you answer? _____

_____

_____

2 Which means nearly the same as **gawking** (paragraph 2)?

▶ **A** staring   ▶ **B** juggling   ▶ **C** thinking   ▶ **D** strolling

What helped you answer? _____

_____

_____

3 This story seems to take place in two settings and times. Explain this.

_____

_____

_____

_____

_____

_____

4 Make an inference to explain Gavin's mixed feelings upon finding himself a knight about to joust.

_____

_____

_____

_____

_____

The Food Festival Celebrity

Read the community story.
Then follow the instructions in the Text-Marking box.

New to the area, and eager to meet their neighbours, the Patel family had a great idea. They would join in with the local summer food festival, and take along a range of delicious snacks that they often made at home together.

They set up their display at the end of the long table. The family was in a jovial mood as they laid out trays of samosas, bhajis, popadums, pickles, paper plates and napkins.

Despite the appealing aroma of the food, few people strolled over, distracted by temptations elsewhere in the food festival tent. With few people to serve, Mrs Patel allowed Deena and Prem to explore. When they returned, ice creams in hand, a commotion grabbed their attention. It was the town's mayor, Julia Brown, and her entourage. They were approaching the Patels' end of the table.

Text Marking

Think about the key events of the story.

◯ Circle four main events in the story.

_____ Underline details about each event.

The mayor stopped and looked at their offerings, smiling warmly as Deena delicately placed some fragrant samosas on a plate, added some popadums and pickles, and served them with a napkin. "Your flavours are fantastic!" the mayor exclaimed, glowing with each mouthful.

Mrs Patel blushed, saying, "Thank you. I'm so glad you're enjoying the food."

Well, that did it. It seemed now that everybody else made a bee-line to the Patel table for samosas. They were newcomers no longer.

The Food Festival Celebrity

▶   **Answer each question. Give details from the community story.**

1   Why did the Patel family set up a table at the local summer food festival?

▶   **A**   They wanted to meet the mayor.

▶   **B**   They wanted to open a restaurant.

▶   **C**   Their house was near the festival tent.

▶   **D**   They hoped it would be a chance to meet their neighbours.

What helped you answer? _____

_____

_____

2   What happened after the mayor tasted the Patels' food?

▶   **A**   Mrs Patel voted for the mayor.   ▶   **C**   The children finished their ice creams.

▶   **B**   Many others came over to try the food.   ▶   **D**   The mayor left to get a drink.

What helped you answer? _____

_____

_____

3   What helped the Patels to stop feeling like newcomers?

_____

_____

_____

_____

_____

4   Explain the meaning of the title. Who is the celebrity at the food festival?

_____

_____

_____

_____

_____

Painted Shoes

Read the crafts story.
Then follow the instructions in the Text-Marking box.

Packing my van by 7am gives me time to get to the lake for this year's craft market. The winding drive will be lovely, as will the reunions with my fellow craftspeople, people I see once a year.

Before coffee and chit-chat, I set up my stall. First, I assemble the lightweight aluminium poles that frame my protective canopy. After all, the market takes place come rain or shine. Then I set up my tables and racks to hold my one-of-a-kind, hand-painted shoes. I put my most popular superhero and cartoon pairs on racks so their designs attract customers. Next, I set out other items – wild laces, funny flip-flops, hair ornaments – neatly in trays. After that, I set out an album showing all my designs for customers to flip through and a sign-up book for people who want to join my mailing list.

Customers start arriving by 11am, so everything must be ready. My last task is to activate and test my Wi-Fi payment machine so I can accept cash and credit cards. At that point, my shoes and I are prepared for the market to open.

I stand most of the day – wearing my favourite shoes – but rarely feel tired. Most shoppers are friendly and curious, which encourages me to talk more about my work. Occasionally, I slip away for a quick snack. At 6pm, when the market closes, I pack, load my van and return home.

Text Marking

Mark the sequence of events in the story.

☐   Box at least seven signal words about sequence and time.

_____   Underline some key events in the painter's day.

1-2-3-4-5   Number the events in order.

Name _____ Date _____

Painted Shoes

▶ **Answer each question. Give details from the crafts story.**

1 Who is telling this story?

▶ **A** a narrator   ▶ **B** a reporter   ▶ **C** the painter   ▶ **D** a customer

What helped you answer? _____

_____

_____

2 Which statement best captures the meaning of **come rain or shine** (paragraph 2)?

▶ **A** Weather is difficult to predict.   ▶ **C** It takes rain and shine for crops to grow.

▶ **B** The event will happen in any weather.   ▶ **D** It never snows in that part of the country.

What helped you answer? _____

_____

_____

3 In what ways are the beginning and the end of day similar for the painter?

_____

_____

_____

_____

_____

4 Make an inference. Think about the events the painter describes.
About when would you expect this person to get home? Explain.

_____

_____

_____

_____

_____

_____

Name _____   Date _____

The Audition

Read the theatre story.
Then follow the instructions in the Text-Marking box.

Wilson is clearly struggling – first he forgot the words to his song, then he took too long between speeches and now he's starting to panic. Recognising his nervousness, the theatre director and the casting director exchange concerned glances and confer softly. First they ask for some water for him. Next they call for a copy of the script to refresh his memory.

While they wait, there is action at the back of the studio. Two performers who had been quietly warming up begin to practise a dazzling routine of break-dancing and acrobatics. They support and catch each other in a range of gravity-defying flips and spins. After completing their stunning routine, both dancers start demonstrating their solo skills, each hoping for a starring role in the show.

Then there is more disappointment for Wilson. The director is so mesmerised by the dancers' performances that she waves Wilson away impatiently. She asks the dancers whether they can sing and act. Moments later, she is signalling for Wilson to leave the studio completely. Then she orders the pianist to start playing the song introduction for the two new hopefuls to show off their voices.

Text Marking

Mark the sequence of events in the story.

☐ Box at least seven signal words about sequence and time.

_____ Underline some key events.

1-2-3-4... Number the events in order.

When Wilson is dismissed, he sidles out of the studio with his head down. Meanwhile, the director gives some encouragement to the next two candidates. Finally she selects the stronger performer and offers him the part, hoping she's made the right choice.

The Audition

▶ **Answer each question. Give details from the theatre story.**

1 What was the first thing that went wrong for Wilson at the audition?

▶ **A** He went to the wrong studio.

▶ **C** He forgot the words to his song.

▶ **B** He was late for the audition.

▶ **D** He tripped over during his dance routine.

What helped you answer? _____

_____

_____

2 Why did the director ask for water and a copy of the script?

▶ **A** She wanted them for Wilson, to help him to calm down.

▶ **B** She felt thirsty and had forgotten what the play was about.

▶ **C** It was hot in the studio.

▶ **D** She needed the items as props for the play.

What helped you answer? _____

_____

_____

3 Make an inference about the director of the play.

_____

_____

_____

_____

4 Summarise the events in this story, focusing on what happened to each character, and how things turned out for them.

_____

_____

_____

_____

_____

_____

Name _____ Date _____

Krishna's Lesson

Read the legend from India.
Then follow the instructions in the Text-Marking box.

Though small and gentle, young Krishna had great wisdom bestowed upon him by Lord Vishnu. In those days, Krishna lived in Vrindavan. Each year, the people there made offerings to Indra, the fierce ruler of clouds and rain, hoping to soothe Indra's temper. Krishna clearly recognised that Indra was neither generous nor sincere; he was selfish and arrogant, unworthy of respect.

To teach Indra a lesson, Krishna addressed the people. "Indra is a bully we need not serve. Instead, it makes more sense to worship Govardhan, our mountain that supports us. Let us honour kind Govardhan, who selflessly shares her lush forests and urges the clouds to shower us." The people approved Krishna's solution.

Indra flew into a mighty rage. "These farmers ignore *me* to worship a mountain on the advice of a child? I shall severely punish this insult," he thundered. Indra ordered the clouds to send furious winds and driving rains to Vrindavan. The tempest terrified the people, who fearfully sought help from young Krishna.

With supreme calm, grace and power, Krishna lifted Govardhan into the air using only the little finger of his left hand. He steadfastly held the mountain like an umbrella, protecting Vrindavan for seven stormy days and nights.

Finally, Indra acknowledged his error. He halted the storm and apologised deeply to Krishna. Thus did humans learn not to give in to disaster.

Text Marking

The story describes a problem. Identify it and read for how it gets solved.

☐ Box these signal words: **temper**, **solution** and **apologised**.

☐ Box the conflict.

___ Underline the resolution.

◯ Circle details about Krishna.

■ SCHOLASTIC

Name _____ Date _____

Krishna's Lesson

▶ **Answer each question. Give details from the legend.**

1 Which term best describes the personality of Indra?

▶ **A** generous ▶ **B** graceful ▶ **C** terrorising ▶ **D** respectful

What helped you answer? _____

_____

_____

2 According to the legend, Vrindavan is _____.

▶ **A** a god ▶ **B** a mountain ▶ **C** a ruler ▶ **D** a village

What helped you answer? _____

_____

_____

3 Why did it take Krishna's help to convince the people to stop honouring Indra?

_____

_____

_____

_____

_____

_____

4 How does the legend make clear that Krishna was wise and honourable?

_____

_____

_____

_____

_____

_____

_____

Name _____ Date _____

Talent Show Contest

Read the entertainment story.
Then follow the instructions in the Text-Marking box.

Ms Spira, the music teacher, had nearly finished auditioning hopefuls for the upcoming talent show. She announced to the two remaining candidates that there was just one spot left to fill, which caused Tameka and Kai to glance nervously at each other across the room. Tameka, a talented dancer, hoped to show off her technique and style in the show, while Kai, a gifted pianist, dreamed of becoming a professional musician and wanted this opportunity to perform. Though each hoped desperately to be selected, that seemed impossible now, with only two more auditions for one place.

Kai moved beside Tameka. "I know you're an awesome dancer, and you know I'm great on the piano. What a shame we've got to battle each other," he whispered.

"Oh, that's kind, but one of us is simply going to be disappointed," Tameka answered.

Kai asked, "What music are you dancing to?" Tameka replied that she planned to dance to the hit, 'Sweet, Fleet Feet'. Kai originally planned to play a classical waltz by Frederic Chopin. But he also knew 'Sweet, Fleet Feet' and could play it energetically, so he suggested something to Tameka that made her grin.

Text Marking

The story describes a problem. Identify it and think about how the characters responded to it and found a way out.

☐ Box the conflict.

◯ Circle the ways that Kai and Tameka reacted to the conflict.

___ Underline the resolution.

Then Ms Spira turned to Tameka and Kai to ask, "Who's next?"

"Both of us – we've become a team!" they responded. The friends chattered as they went onto the stage. "May we please have a few moments to warm up?" Tameka asked politely.

Name _____ Date _____

Talent Show Contest

▶ **Answer each question. Give details from the entertainment story.**

1 Who is telling the story?

▶ **A** Ms Spira ▶ **B** Tameka ▶ **C** Kai ▶ **D** a narrator

What helped you answer? _____

_____

_____

2 Two words that could describe everyone auditioning for the talent show are...

▶ **A** dancers and pianists. ▶ **C** hopefuls and candidates.

▶ **B** best friends and hopefuls. ▶ **D** jugglers and musicians.

What helped you answer? _____

_____

_____

3 Why did Tameka ask Ms Spira for a few moments to warm up?

_____

_____

_____

_____

_____

_____

4 What inferences can you make about Kai based on his idea?

_____

_____

_____

_____

_____

_____

Name _____ Date _____

The Unlucky Lizard

Read the African-American folktale.
Then follow the instructions in the Text-Marking box.

Ages back, Lizard and Frog both sat upright like dogs. Then came the day that things changed forever for Lizard. The pair were strolling along a dusty path near their swamp. Around a bend they noticed a lush green field with a clear blue pond. They yearned for a visit, but a sturdy wooden fence blocked the way.

"I'd love a swim in that sweet water," said Frog longingly.

"I'd love to catch some fine insects there," pined Lizard.

So the two approached the fence, which seemed to grow taller and more threatening with each step. To make things worse, the fence boards fitted snugly together and were buried deep in the ground. They saw no possibility to clamber over or dig under.

Frog and Lizard sat upright like dogs by that frustrating fence, pondering how to get to the other side. Then Frog spied a thin crevice near the ground. "I'm going to squeeze myself through," he announced. So he shoved and squirmed and wriggled until he popped out on the other side!

"Your turn, Lizard," Frog yelled. So Lizard scuttled to the crack. He pressed and squashed and struggled to get through. He pushed so hard that a fence board tumbled and flattened him. After that, Lizard never again sat like a dog, but could only slither close to the ground. Frog and Lizard remained friends despite Lizards' flatter appearance.

Text Marking

Use context clues to unlock meaning.

○ Circle the words: **longingly**, **clamber** and **crevice**.

▭ Box the expression: **hankered for**.

___ Underline context clues for each of the words and the phrase.

The Unlucky Lizard

▶ **Answer each question. Give details from the folktale.**

1 If you were to **clamber** over something (paragraph 4), you would most likely be…

▶ **A** arguing.   ▶ **B** climbing.   ▶ **C** slithering.   ▶ **D** wondering.

What helped you answer? _____

_____

2 According to this folktale, what did Frog and Lizard share a **yearning** for (paragraph 1)?

▶ **A** making new friends   ▶ **C** sitting upright like dogs can

▶ **B** having a refreshing swim   ▶ **D** getting past a fence to a field and pond

What helped you answer? _____

_____

3 Describe a situation when using the word **longingly** makes sense (paragraph 2).

_____

_____

_____

_____

_____

4 What lesson do you think Lizard might have learned from this tale?

_____

_____

_____

_____

_____

Name _____ Date _____

The Shipwreck

Read the fable, adapted from Aesop.
Then follow the instructions in the Text-Marking box.

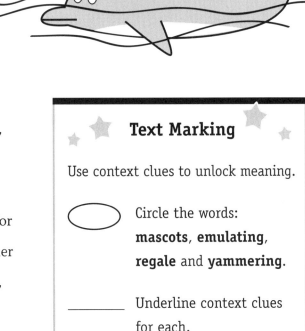

Long ago, when dolphins were friendly towards humans, shipwrecked sailors often told of being rescued by holding onto a dolphin's fin to get back to shore. Also at that time, ships commonly carried animal mascots, like monkeys, who were known to be clever, entertaining companions, and good at mimicking the sailors.

One stormy night near Athens, Greece, a ship broke apart, dumping its sailors into the sea. Struggling, they grabbed onto anything they could to stay afloat. Emulating them, the monkey clung to an oar.

A dolphin swimming past, mistaking the monkey for a sailor, invited him to climb onto her back and grasp her tightly while she carried him to land. She politely asked, "Are you from Greece?"

"Yes, my family is from Athens," replied the monkey.

"You sound like a well-educated person," said the dolphin respectfully. So the monkey began to regale her with fantastical tales; but all were lies. Soon the dolphin interrupted the monkey's yammering to indicate land on the horizon.

"As an Athenian," the dolphin said, "you must surely know Piraeus."

"Naturally!" the monkey replied. "Piraeus is my father's first cousin, whom we visit often because he is our favourite relative."

Knowing that Piraeus was the port nearest Athens, the dolphin realised the monkey was an imposter. So she dived under the waves, letting the monkey swim on his own, and sought an honest man to save.

Text Marking

Use context clues to unlock meaning.

◯ Circle the words:
mascots, **emulating**, **regale** and **yammering**.

_____ Underline context clues for each.

Name _____ Date _____

The Shipwreck

▶ **Answer each question. Give details from the fable.**

1 Which word is a synonym for **mimicking** (paragraph 1)?

▶ **A** realising ▶ **B** emulating ▶ **C** yammering ▶ **D** entertaining

What helped you answer? _____

_____

_____

2 Which is the most appropriate moral for this fable?

▶ **A** Look before you leap. ▶ **C** A liar deceives no one but himself.

▶ **B** The memory of a good deed lives. ▶ **D** A friend in need is a friend indeed.

What helped you answer? _____

_____

_____

3 According to this fable, why did sailors bring animals aboard ship?

_____

_____

_____

_____

_____

_____

4 Why did the dolphin dive under the waves at the end?

_____

_____

_____

_____

_____

_____

_____

Room and Bored

Read the family story.
Then follow the instructions in the Text-Marking box.

Luckily, Kenji has his own bedroom, but he had outgrown it. About to enter secondary school, why would he want a room with a kiddie desk and dinosaur curtains? With that in mind, Kenji asked his parents if he could bring his room up to date. To his delight, they agreed and together they examined the room with an eye for how they could renovate it.

The bed was the first thing to go, replaced by a bunk bed for sleepover guests. Its duvet cover, decorated with cartoon animals, also had to go. "Footballs might be better," Kenji suggested. His mother agreed to shop for different curtains, too.

Similarly, the tiny desk had outlived its use; a new computer station would provide a welcome contrast. The watercolour paintings on the wall, which he'd made in Year 4, also had to go, along with the pirate toy chest. Rather, he'd hang up pictures of tennis players he admired and get a bookcase.

On the other hand, Kenji was content with his room's pale green colour. "That's the same colour as the seats at the stadium," he explained. And the rug was okay, he thought, despite its stains.

When the upgrade was completed, the change in the character of the room was apparent. At peace in his more mature environment, Kenji felt ready for his new school.

Text Marking

Compare and contrast the before-and-after appearances of Kenji's room.

☐ Box signal words for comparing and contrasting.

⬭ Circle the ways the room will stay the same.

___ Underline the ways it will be different.

Name _____ Date _____

Room and Bored

▶ **Answer each question. Give details from the family story.**

1 What does Kenji mean by asking to bring his room **up to date** (paragraph 1)?

▶ **A** Hang pictures of fast athletes.   ▶ **C** Make it age-appropriate.

▶ **B** Fill it with newer furniture.   ▶ **D** Fix it up quickly.

What helped you answer? _____

_____

_____

2 Which is a synonym for **renovate** (paragraph 1)?

▶ **A** upgrade   ▶ **B** keep the same   ▶ **C** tidy up   ▶ **D** remove

What helped you answer? _____

_____

_____

3 Summarise the change in character of the before-and-after versions of Kenji's room.

_____

_____

_____

_____

_____

_____

4 What theme does this story explore?

_____

_____

_____

_____

_____

_____

_____

_____

Name _____ Date _____

The Chapman Stick

Read the music story.
Then follow the instructions in the Text-Marking box.

At the music museum, I got to see new and ancient instruments from around the world. They were all quite fascinating. Then I learned that there was going to be a demonstration of a special instrument called a Chapman Stick.

"Good afternoon," said a musician. "Please welcome my band." I was puzzled, because he was by himself. There weren't any other band members on stage beside him. He held something that looked like a guitar, only it didn't have a body. The entire instrument consisted of just a fretboard, which was wider and longer than a guitar's fretboard. It had more strings than a guitar, too.

He plugged the Chapman Stick into an electric amplifier, just like a guitar. Then he began to play. I couldn't believe my ears. I was amazed by all the different sounds the Chapman Stick could make. The instrument sounded like a guitar, a piano, a bass and a drum, all at the same time. I enjoyed hearing the musician play full songs all by himself.

I wish I had a Chapman Stick. I could be a one-boy band. I know what I'm requesting for my birthday this year!

Text Marking

Compare and contrast the Chapman Stick with an electric guitar.

☐ Box signal words for comparing and contrasting.

⬭ Circle the ways the instruments are alike.

___ Underline the ways they are different.

Name _____ Date _____

The Chapman Stick

▶ **Answer each question. Give details from the music story.**

1 Something that is **ancient** (paragraph 1) must be _____.

▶ **A** electronic ▶ **B** very old ▶ **C** musical ▶ **D** unique

What helped you answer? _____

_____

_____

2 From whose point of view is this story told?

▶ **A** the musician ▶ **B** a museum guide ▶ **C** a museum visitor ▶ **D** a pianist

What helped you answer? _____

_____

_____

3 What inference can you make about the storyteller?

_____

_____

_____

_____

_____

_____

4 Look at the illustration. Compare and contrast the fretboards of the Chapman Stick with the electric guitar.

_____

_____

_____

_____

_____

_____

_____

_____

Name _____ Date _____

Have You Ever Seen?

Read the poem.
Then follow the instructions in the Text-Marking box.

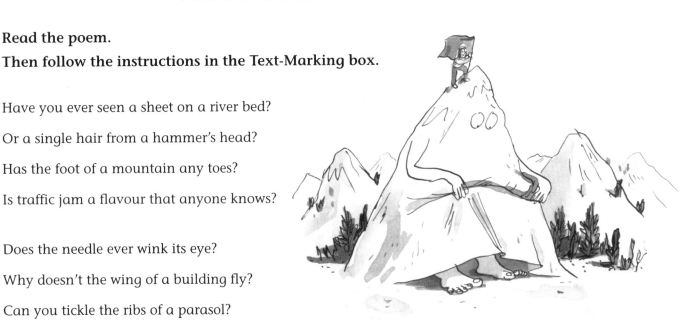

Have you ever seen a sheet on a river bed?

Or a single hair from a hammer's head?

Has the foot of a mountain any toes?

Is traffic jam a flavour that anyone knows?

Does the needle ever wink its eye?

Why doesn't the wing of a building fly?

Can you tickle the ribs of a parasol?

Or open the trunk of a tree at all?

Are the teeth of a rake ever going to bite?

Have the hands of a clock any left or right?

Can the garden plot be deep and dark?

And what is the sound of a birch's bark?

Writers use **figurative language**
to describe one thing by comparing
it with something else.

Examples: • a *carpet* of flowers
            • a *blanket* of fog

Text Marking

Make an inference: What makes
this poem amusing and interesting?

X   Cross a box to show the
        literary strategy the poet uses
        throughout.

☐ flashback

☐ exaggeration

☐ figurative language

_____ Underline words or phrases
in each line that have
multiple meanings.

Think about what you
already know.

Have You Ever Seen?

▶ Answer each question. Give details from the poem.

1   Which type of **jam** does the poet joke about in the first stanza?

▶ **A** hold-up   ▶ **B** squash   ▶ **C** fruit   ▶ **D** play music

What helped you answer? _____

_____

_____

2   Where would you be most likely to find a **deep and dark plot** (stanza 3)?

▶ **A** on a hike   ▶ **B** on a graph   ▶ **C** in a garden   ▶ **D** in a mystery

What helped you answer? _____

_____

_____

3   In your own words, what point is the poet trying to get across?

_____

_____

_____

_____

_____

_____

4   Why does each line in this poem ask a question without ever giving an answer?

_____

_____

_____

_____

_____

_____

_____

To Go or Not to Go

Read the science-fiction story.
Then follow the instructions in the Text-Marking box.

"It's the opportunity of a lifetime, Rashid. We'll be pioneers!" said Dr Donovan.

Despite his mother's enthusiasm, Rashid wasn't convinced that joining a new colony on Mars was a good idea. "But Mum," he said, "we'd have to stay there at *least* two years. And when you add on the six months or more it will take to get there and the same to return, we'd be away from home and friends for three years – or longer! It'll be 2051 when we finally get back, and I'll be sixteen already!"

"But Rashid, just think of the advantages, not the least of which is how much time we'll spend together as a family."

Unconvinced, Rashid responded, "Mum, taking this trip is not only unappealing, but probably unhealthy, too. We'll be exposed to deep-space radiation. Plus, life in that planet's low-gravity environment might be too weird. For instance, what will we do for entertainment? I don't expect we'll find swimming pools, rugby pitches or restaurants!"

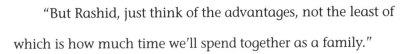

Text Marking

Make an inference: How does the story reveal the personalities of Rashid and his mother?

_____ Underline text clues.

 Think about what you already know.

Rashid's mother knew all this, but she was passionate about going, believing that after preparation and study, they could meet each potential challenge. "Just think how exciting it would be, darling," she replied, "an experience like no other. How can I encourage you to be as excited as I am about this chance for adventure?"

"I'm not that excited about bringing back Martian microbes, Mum. Can I go to rugby practice now?"

To Go or Not to Go

▶ Answer each question. Give details from the science-fiction story.

1 Something is **the opportunity of a lifetime** (paragraph 1) if it is _____.

▶ **A** challenging   ▶ **B** dangerous   ▶ **C** lively   ▶ **D** rare

What helped you answer? _____

_____

_____

2 Which description best fits Dr Donovan?

▶ **A** argumentative   ▶ **B** cautious   ▶ **C** passionate   ▶ **D** timid

What helped you answer? _____

_____

_____

3 Based on the story, what kind of person is Rashid? In what ways is his personality different from his mother's?

_____

_____

_____

_____

_____

_____

4 What details in the story indicate that it is a work of science fiction?

_____

_____

_____

_____

_____

_____

_____

Name _____ Date _____

Egg of Chaos

Read the Chinese creation myth.
Then follow the instructions in the Text-Marking box.

At first, the universe was jumbled inside a huge egg. That murky chaos contained all forms of opposites, or *yin* and *yang*. In the whirling mixture were water and fire, night and day, north and south and so on. And there was Pangu, the being who would one day create our world.

Pangu slept inside the egg of chaos for 18,000 years. During that time, the *yin* and *yang* of all things was tangled together. He separated the heavier *yin* from the lighter *yang*. The *yang* floated up to become the sky while the *yin* settled to become the earth.

Standing between the two parts, Pangu's head touched sky and his feet strode upon earth. Over the next 18,000 years, sky and earth grew ever more vast, moving apart by two metres each day.

Pangu also grew, keeping sky and earth separated. By the time of his death, earth and sky had settled into their places. One of Pangu's eyes became the sun, the other the moon. His breath became wind and clouds; his voice turned into the sound of thunder. Pangu's body formed great mountains and his blood its flowing waters. His veins became roads and his muscles fertile fields. His hairs remained in the sky as glittering stars.

Text Marking

Summarise the story.

  Circle the main idea of the story.

_____ Underline important details.

Name _____ Date _____

Egg of Chaos

▶ **Answer each question. Give details from the creation myth.**

1 Which best describes the concept of **yin** and **yang** (paragraph 1)?

▶ **A** powers of creation   ▶ **B** entanglement   ▶ **C** opposites   ▶ **D** chaos

What helped you answer? _____

_____

_____

2 How did earth and sky stay separated?

▶ **A** The egg of chaos expanded.   ▶ **C** Earth and sky grew two metres each day.

▶ **B** Pangu grew and kept them apart.   ▶ **D** The myth does not explain this.

What helped you answer? _____

_____

_____

3 According to Chinese belief, *yin* and *yang* are opposite forces that are also related in some way. Explain how health and sickness are examples of *yin* and *yang*.

_____

_____

_____

_____

_____

_____

4 Summarise how the actions of Pangu influenced how the world came to be.

_____

_____

_____

_____

_____

_____

Febold Feboldson's Find

Read this tall tale from the American Midwest.
Then follow the instructions in the Text-Marking box.

Have you ever seen a popcorn ball? It's a popular American snack, made of popcorn pieces stuck together with syrup and formed into a clump. You might imagine some clever cook thought of this delicious idea. Well, that's NOT how popcorn balls came to exist, at least according to old Febold Feboldson. He claimed that the popcorn ball invented itself during the weird summer of 1874.

Farmers in the American Midwest called that growing season The Year of Striped Weather. That's because it alternated rainy and hot, not day by day, but by sections of cropland. Fields grew in stripes: first you'd see 1.5km-wide stripe of crops wilting in the searing heat, then a 1.5km-wide stripe of waterlogged crops soaking nearly to death.

This was exactly the situation on Febold Feboldson's farm. He grew sweetcorn down in the Dismal River valley and sugar cane up on the hills above. One day the sun baked his sweetcorn plants so much that the kernels popped,

Text Marking

Summarise the story.
Think about its theme.

◯ Circle the main idea of the story.

____ Underline important details.

causing a yellow blizzard of popcorn. Meanwhile, the rain was drenching his sugar-cane stalks so badly that the syrup inside washed out and flowed down towards the popcorn. A ball soon formed, growing gigantic as it tumbled along. Febold estimated that it was about 60 metres wide!

Febold's neighbour, Bert Bergstrom, witnessed this eye-popping event. Bert offered to help Febold to roll the great popcorn ball into town to impress visitors. But just then, a swarm of hungry grasshoppers devoured the entire very-first popcorn ball.

MSCHOLASTIC

Name _____ Date _____

Febold Feboldson's Find

▶ **Answer each question. Give details from the tall tale.**

1 What odd thing happened during The Year of Striped Weather?

▶ **A** Strange weather made crops grow in striped sections.

▶ **B** Farmers planted their crops only at night.

▶ **C** The only crops that grew had stripes on them.

▶ **D** Febold Feboldson met Bert Bergstrom.

What helped you answer? _____

_____

_____

2 Which word does NOT mean the same as the other three?

▶ **A** soaked   ▶ **B** drenched   ▶ **C** tumbled   ▶ **D** waterlogged

What helped you answer? _____

_____

_____

3 Explain the meaning of the title of this passage.

_____

_____

_____

_____

4 Why do you think the tall tale ends with grasshoppers devouring the entire popcorn ball?

_____

_____

_____

_____

_____

_____

_____

Answers

◀ Sample Text Markings

Passage 1: Fishing With Grandpa Leon

1 D; *Sample answer:* I picked D because it's the only answer that makes sense, and I found a context clue in the first paragraph.

2 A; *Sample answer:* I picked A because Grandpa Leon seems upbeat and hopeful about the fishing trip.

3 *Sample answer:* I think Ronan would say that the trip had many long boring stretches because the fish weren't biting, but he was entertained by Grandpa Leon's stories and did enjoy making the first 'catch'.

4 *Sample answer:* He acted as if the suitcase itself was a prized catch and didn't seem the least bit disappointed.

◀ Sample Text Markings

Passage 2: Operation Pied Piper, 1940

1 D; *Sample answer:* I picked D because I could tell that the story was told in the third person.

2 B; *Sample answer:* I picked B because I understood in paragraph 1 that children were evacuated for their own safety, and refugees are also people who are escaping from danger and need a safe place to stay.

3 *Sample answer:* I think Miss Burrows is a kind, gentle and caring person, but also quite strict.

4 *Sample answer:* The opening paragraph provides some historical background about the time and place where the story is set.

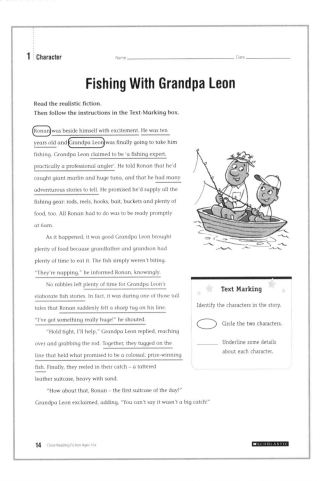

■SCHOLASTIC

The Worksheet Page

The Expedition

Read the adventure story.
Then follow the instructions in the Text-Marking box.

They'd been trapped by ice for 36 days and had been on their own for longer than that, ever since a storm separated them from the ship and the rest of the crew on their expedition. Karl was in a pitiful state – lost, weak, frightened and shivering from unrelenting cold. He was also suffering the painful effects of frostbite.

Suddenly, ice cracked enough for the boat to break loose and begin to bob gently in the frigid sea. The crew cheered their good fortune. No longer stuck in the ice, their chances of survival had edged up a notch. But Karl understood that the struggles had not ended, as medical supplies were nearly gone and there was barely any food left. If that weren't terrifying enough, the maps were lost, too.

The crew navigated icy waters until their hands bled and muscles ached. For days, Karl saw nothing in the muted, constant light but other ice floes. Then, finally, he detected a sound in the stillness that he hadn't heard for months: the cawing of birds. That sweet sound signalled that land was near. All were exhilarated!

The land they found was snow-covered and flat. The crew rowed along its barren coast until they spotted the mouth of a river. Karl and the men entered, presuming it would lead to a village and safety. On they plodded, ever more hopeful of survival.

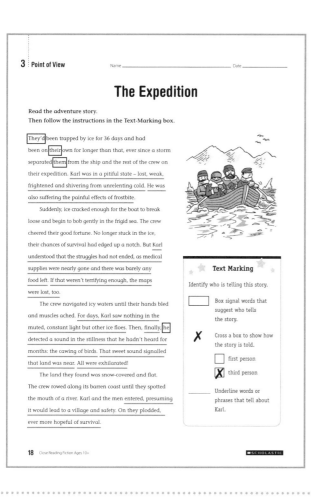

Text Marking

Identify who is telling this story.

☐ Box signal words that suggest who tells the story.

✗ Cross a box to show how the story is told.

☐ first person
☒ third person

___ Underline words or phrases that tell about Karl.

SCHOLASTIC

The Record Setter

Read the humorous story.
Then follow the instructions in the Text-Marking box.

My brother, Alex, is generally considered to be a reliable, clever, thoughtful fellow. I say 'generally' because of things like what he's doing right now.

Picture this and you'll understand. While I, Nate, sit here playing a video game and texting with half my friends – two perfectly normal things to be doing for amusement – what is he occupied with? Alex is standing over there, counting softly to himself 79, 80, 81, 82… while he repeatedly bats a rubber ball attached by an elastic string to a wooden paddle. This is nonsensical behaviour, is it not?

You might think I'm being too hard on Alex, as brothers sometimes can be to one another. On the contrary, I'm being lenient. You see, this time it's paddle-ball batting, but the last time – and I refer to just a few weeks ago – the challenge was standing on his head for as long as he could, with a timer set up on the rug. Of course, he had to read it upside down, but I suppose he got better at it day by day. Maybe he should've put the timer upside down, too.

Frankly, I'm getting a bit concerned. What if one of his weird pals introduces him to alligator wrestling? Or what if he gets enticed to take up tightrope walking from skyscraper to skyscraper? I tell you, for Alex, these ideas are not too far-fetched!

Text Marking

Identify the main character in this story. Read for clues about point of view.

☐ Box signal words that suggest who tells the story.

✗ Cross a box to show how the story is told.

☒ first person
☐ third person

◯ Circle the name of the main character.

___ Underline words or phrases that describe the main character.

SCHOLASTIC

Answer Key Column

◀ **Sample Text Markings**

Passage 3: The Expedition

1 C; *Sample answer:* I picked C because although the story includes boats, nature and weather, the main issue in the story is whether, when and how the crew will survive their terrible and challenging ordeal.

2 A; *Sample answer:* I picked A because I understood that the crew had been in a very cold situation for a long time, and *constant* is the best synonym.

3 *Sample answer:* The narrator knew that although circumstances had improved, survival was still uncertain.

4 *Sample answer:* I think the story takes place in a very cold climate, perhaps in the Arctic Sea, because there is ice, frozen for long stretches, barren lands and near-constant light.

◀ **Sample Text Markings**

Passage 4: The Record Setter

1 D; *Sample answer:* I picked D because Nate says in the second paragraph that he likes playing video games and considers that normal behaviour.

2 A; *Sample answer:* I picked A because 'easygoing' seems to be the opposite of being too hard on Alex.

3 *Sample answer:* Although Alex may do things that Nate finds peculiar, Alex probably has no intention of taking up alligator wrestling or tightrope walking.

4 *Sample answer:* Alex might poke fun at Nate for all the time he wastes on video games and texting with his friends.

Answers

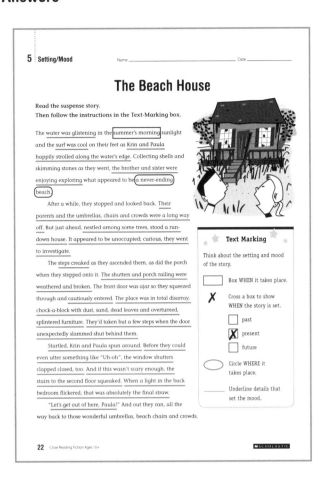

5 Setting/Mood　　Name ＿＿＿＿＿＿＿＿　Date ＿＿＿＿＿＿＿

The Beach House

Read the suspense story.
Then follow the instructions in the Text-Marking box.

The water was glistening in the summer's morning sunlight and the surf was cool on their feet as Krin and Paula happily strolled along the water's edge. Collecting shells and skimming stones as they went, the brother and sister were enjoying exploring what appeared to be a never-ending beach.

After a while, they stopped and looked back. Their parents and the umbrellas, chairs and crowds were a long way off. But just ahead, nestled among some trees, stood a run-down house. It appeared to be unoccupied; curious, they went to investigate.

The steps creaked as they ascended them, as did the porch when they stepped onto it. The shutters and porch railing were weathered and broken. The front door was ajar so they squeezed through and cautiously entered. The place was in total disarray, chock-a-block with dust, sand, dead leaves and overturned, splintered furniture. They'd taken but a few steps when the door unexpectedly slammed shut behind them.

Startled, Krin and Paula spun around. Before they could even utter something like "Uh-oh", the window shutters clapped closed, too. And if this wasn't scary enough, the stairs to the second floor squeaked. When a light in the back bedroom flickered, that was absolutely the final straw.

"Let's get out of here, Paula!" And out they ran, all the way back to those wonderful umbrellas, beach chairs and crowds.

Text Marking

Think about the setting and mood of the story.

☐ Box WHEN it takes place.

✗ Cross a box to show WHEN the story is set.

☐ past
☒ present
☐ future

◯ Circle WHERE it takes place.

＿ Underline details that set the mood.

◀ Sample Text Markings

Passage 5: The Beach House

1 C; *Sample answer:* I picked C because I could tell that it is written in third person ('he', 'they') and it probably wasn't told by a ghost.

2 B; *Sample answer:* I picked B because according to the description, the inside of the house is full of lots of stuff.

3 *Sample answer:* I think the haunted house scared them a lot, which made them grateful to be safely back among their parents and the crowds on the beach.

4 *Sample answer:* The story is set on a long beach on a summer morning. At first, the mood is pleasant as the two happy strollers are enjoying a lovely, relaxing day. The mood turns more creepy and scary when the pair enter a vacant house that unexpectedly seems haunted.

---

6 Setting/Mood　　Name ＿＿＿＿＿＿＿　Date ＿＿＿＿＿＿＿

Mile-and-a-Quarter Monkey

Read the descriptive story.
Then follow the instructions in the Text-Marking box.

It had taken us nearly five hours from the river to reach Three-Mile House that hot summer day in the Grand Canyon. We were already tiring from the hike, and knowing that a relentlessly uphill slog still lay ahead, we gratefully rested there.

The path wound upwards through awesome – in the true sense of the word – scenery, rich with spectacular rock formations. The other hikers in the hut, also fatigued from their challenging climbs, seemed in an upbeat mood. Eventually, we gathered our courage to resume the twisting path to the rim.

Mile-and-a-Half House was our next stopping point, and reaching it was a steady struggle. Our muscles ached, our gusto was diminished and we were drained upon arrival. After a much-appreciated second rest, longer than our first, we reluctantly began the final leg of our ascent.

The hike was not getting any easier in the heat, and we paused continuously. While wishing the trek were over, we spotted it overhead: an immense monkey face! That's precisely what the eroded rocks looked like. We excitedly told everyone we passed about where to see Mile-and-a-Quarter Monkey, as we named it. Each hiker gladly promised to keep a lookout for it. Suddenly, amazingly, we felt a renewed bounce in our step. Discovering the giant monkey face had put wings on our feet. Energised, we practically flew out of the canyon, and that was awesome, too.

Text Marking

Think about the setting and mood of the story.

☐ Box WHEN it takes place.

◯ Circle WHERE it takes place.

✗ Cross a box to show the setting.

☒ realistic
☐ imaginary

＿ Underline details that set the mood.

◀ Sample Text Markings

Passage 6: Mile-and-a-Quarter Monkey

1 C; *Sample answer:* I picked C since the hikers were in a grumpy mood because they were so hot and tired, even though they were having a great hike.

2 B; *Sample answer:* I picked B because I gathered from the story that the hike, also called a trek, was strenuous and exhausting, much like a lengthy hike in snow.

3 *Sample answer:* The hikers walked in the hot summer heat on a path that was steep, winding and uphill.

4 *Sample answer:* Noticing a rock formation that looked like a giant monkey was a funny discovery, which lifted the spirits of the hikers and gave them an energy boost.

■ SCHOLASTIC

◀ **Sample Text Markings**

Passage 7: Medieval Festival

1 C; *Sample answer:* I picked C because this is the most logical choice.

2 A; *Sample answer:* I picked A because I pictured Gavin trying to take in all the sights and not paying attention, which is probably why he tripped.

3 *Sample answer:* The story starts out in the present, with Gavin and his mum attending a Medieval Festival. But his fall seems to cause him to travel back into medieval times, where he isn't a child but is suddenly a knight jousting for his queen.

4 *Sample answer:* Although Gavin was interested in seeing a joust performed, it's a completely different experience to actually participate in such a dangerous and fierce physical competition.

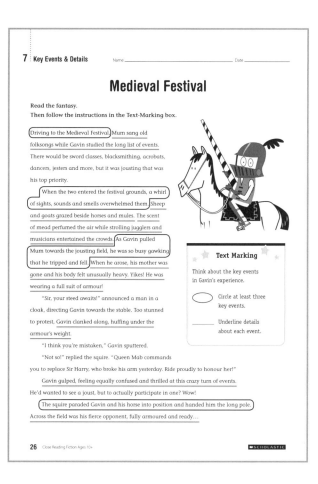

◀ **Sample Text Markings**

Passage 8: The Food Festival Celebrity

1 D; *Sample answer:* I picked D because it says that the Patels are new in the area and eager to meet their neighbours.

2 B; *Sample answer:* I picked B because it says that in the last paragraph.

3 *Sample answer:* Their samosas and other dishes helped them to meet their neighbours and to feel like part of their new community.

4 *Sample answer:* Although the mayor seems to be the celebrity, the true celebrity is actually Mrs Patel because of the quality of her samosas.

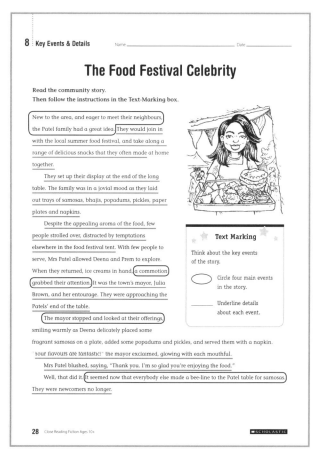

Answers

Sample Text Markings

Passage 9: Painted Shoes

1 C; *Sample answer:* I picked C because I could tell that the story is told in the first person because of the use of 'I', 'me' and 'my'.

2 B; *Sample answer:* I picked B because I know this expression. It's like 'the show must go on'. The event will happen no matter what.

3 *Sample answer:* Both involve transporting the painted shoes and other kit to or from the market. Both ends of the day require the painter to pack or unpack the goods, set up or take down the booth, and pack or unpack the van for travel.

4 *Sample answer:* The painter leaves home by 7am in order to get ready for the customers who will show up four hours later. The market ends by 6pm, so I'm guessing it will take a similar amount of time to pack up as it did to set up, plus driving time. So the painter will probably get home around 10pm.

Sample Text Markings

Passage 10: The Audition

1 C; *Sample answer:* I picked C, because the first sentence says that he forgot his words to the song.

2 A; *Sample answer:* I picked A because paragraph one says that the director realised Wilson was nervous and was concerned about him.

3 *Sample answer:* I think the director understands how anxious people can get at an audition, but she is not worried about hurting people's feelings and she just focuses on getting the best performers for her show.

4 *Sample answer:* Wilson had an audition. He didn't do well, and he was sent away when the director noticed some better performers. He didn't get the part.

The director was holding auditions. The first candidate didn't do well. The next two candidates were better, and she gave one of them the part.

Two dancers were practising at an audition. The director noticed them and asked them to sing. One of them got the part.

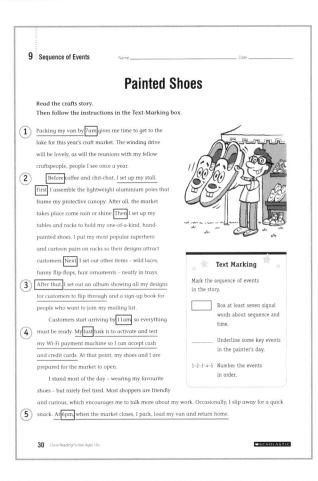

Krishna's Lesson

Read the legend from India.
Then follow the instructions in the Text-Marking box.

Though small and gentle, young Krishna had great wisdom bestowed upon him by Lord Vishnu. In those days, Krishna lived in Vrindavan. Each year, the people there made offerings to Indra, the fierce ruler of clouds and rain, hoping to soothe Indra's temper. Krishna clearly recognised that Indra was neither generous nor sincere; he was selfish and arrogant, unworthy of respect.

To teach Indra a lesson, Krishna addressed the people. "Indra is a bully we need not serve. Instead, it makes more sense to worship Govardhan, our mountain that supports us. Let us honour kind Govardhan, who selflessly shares her lush forests and urges the clouds to shower us." The people approved Krishna's solution.

Indra flew into a mighty rage. "These farmers ignore *me* to worship a mountain on the advice of a child? I shall severely punish this insult," he thundered. Indra ordered the clouds to send furious winds and driving rains to Vrindavan. The tempest terrified the people, who fearfully sought help from young Krishna.

With supreme calm, grace and power, Krishna lifted Govardhan into the air using only the little finger of his left hand. He steadfastly held the mountain like an umbrella, protecting Vrindavan for seven stormy days and nights.

Finally, Indra acknowledged his error. He halted the storm and apologised deeply to Krishna. Thus did humans learn not to give in to disaster.

Text Marking

The story describes a problem. Identify it and read for how it gets solved.

☐ Box these signal words: **temper**, **solution** and **apologised**.

☐ Box the conflict.

___ Underline the resolution.

⬭ Circle details about Krishna.

◀ Sample Text Markings

Passage 11: Krishna's Lesson

1 C; *Sample answer:* I picked C because Indra's actions frighten the people, who fear his temper.

2 D; *Sample answer:* I picked D because the details of the story made it clear that Vrindavan was a place where people lived, not a person or god.

3 *Sample answer:* The people feared Indra and hoped that their offerings would keep his temper under control. But when Krishna proposed a new plan, they were willing to try his solution.

4 *Sample answer:* Krishna was gentle, possessed wisdom from Lord Vishnu, cared about the people of Vrindavan, justified the changes he suggested and steadfastly protected the people during the storm until Indra gave in and apologised.

Talent Show Contest

Read the entertainment story.
Then follow the instructions in the Text-Marking box.

Ms Spira, the music teacher, had nearly finished auditioning hopefuls for the upcoming talent show. She announced to the two remaining candidates that there was just one spot left to fill, which caused Tameka and Kai to glance nervously at each other across the room. Tameka, a talented dancer, hoped to show off her technique and style in the show, while Kai, a gifted pianist, dreamed of becoming a professional musician and wanted this opportunity to perform. Though each hoped desperately to be selected, that seemed impossible now, with only two more auditions for one place.

Kai moved beside Tameka. "I know you're an awesome dancer, and you know I'm great on the piano. What a shame we've got to battle each other," he whispered.

"Oh, that's kind, but one of us is simply going to be disappointed," Tameka answered.

Kai asked, "What music are you dancing to?" Tameka replied that she planned to dance to the hit, 'Sweet, Fleet Feet'. Kai originally planned to play a classical waltz by Frederic Chopin. But he also knew 'Sweet, Fleet Feet' and could play it energetically, so he suggested something to Tameka that made her grin.

Then Ms Spira turned to Tameka and Kai to ask, "Who's next?"

"Both of us – we've become a team!" they responded. The friends chattered as they went onto the stage. "May we please have a few moments to warm up?" Tameka asked politely.

Text Marking

The story describes a problem. Identify it and think about how the characters responded to it and found a way out.

☐ Box the conflict.

⬭ Circle the ways that Kai and Tameka reacted to the conflict.

___ Underline the resolution.

◀ Sample Text Markings

Passage 12: Talent Show Contest

1 D; *Sample answer:* I picked D because I could tell the piece was written in the third person, so it was told by a narrator.

2 C; *Sample answer:* I read both of those words in the first paragraph and understood that both described children hoping to be chosen for the talent show.

3 *Sample answer:* I think Tameka was hoping for extra time to practise with Kai before the audition.

4 *Sample answer:* Kai must feel confident enough about his musical skills to switch to a different piece at the last minute. He also must have believed that teaming up with a talented dancer would increase their chances at the talent show.

Answers

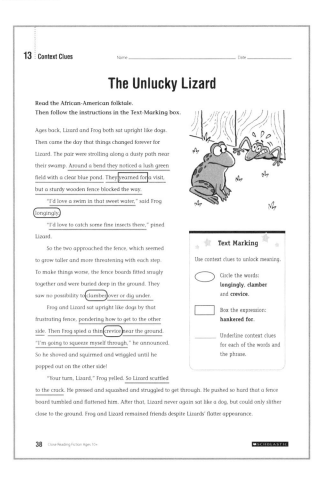

◀ Sample Text Markings

Passage 13: The Unlucky Lizard

1 B; *Sample answer:* I picked B because I worked out from the sentence that 'dig under' was the opposite, so 'clambering' must mean climbing over.

2 D; *Sample answer:* I picked D because the main idea of the story is their desire to get beyond that fence to the lush green field and clear blue pond.

3 *Sample answer:* I would use the word 'longingly' to describe how I might want something badly while knowing it might be hard to come by. I might ask 'longingly' to visit a faraway place.

4 *Sample answer:* He might have learned not to try to go where he wasn't wanted, or not to let a friend dare him to do something dangerous.

◀ Sample Text Markings

Passage 14: The Shipwreck

1 B; *Sample answer:* I picked B because I found the word *emulating* later on in the fable and I think it means the same.

2 C; *Sample answer:* I picked C because the monkey was a liar whose lies lost him the help of the dolphin.

3 *Sample answer:* The fable explains that the sailors enjoyed having some sort of mascot because it provided entertainment for them.

4 *Sample answer:* She did this to get the monkey off her back after realising that he was a liar. She preferred to save an honest person.

SCHOLASTIC

Name _____ Date _____

Room and Bored

Read the family story.
Then follow the instructions in the Text-Marking box.

Luckily, Kenji has his own bedroom, but he had outgrown it. About to enter secondary school, why would he want a room with a kiddie desk and dinosaur curtains? With that in mind, Kenji asked his parents if he could bring his room up to date. To his delight, they agreed and together they examined the room with an eye for how they could renovate it.

The bed was the first thing to go, replaced by a bunk bed for sleepover guests. Its duvet cover, decorated with cartoon animals, also had to go. "Footballs might be better," Kenji suggested. His mother agreed to shop for different curtains, too.

Similarly, the tiny desk had outlived its use; a new computer station would provide a welcome contrast. The watercolour paintings on the wall, which he'd made in Year 4, also had to go, along with the pirate toy chest. Rather, he'd hang up pictures of tennis players he admired and get a bookcase.

On the other hand, Kenji was content with his room's pale green colour. "That's the same colour as the seats at the stadium," he explained. And the rug was okay, he thought, despite its stains.

When the upgrade was completed, the change in the character of the room was apparent. At peace in his more mature environment, Kenji felt ready for his new school.

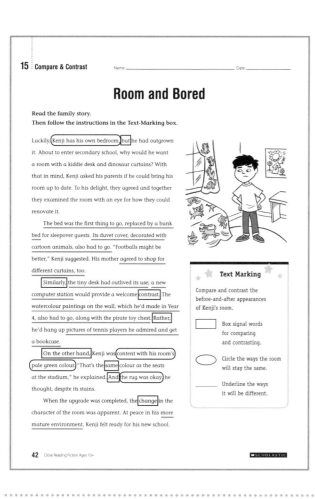

Text Marking

Compare and contrast the before-and-after appearances of Kenji's room.

☐ Box signal words for comparing and contrasting.

◯ Circle the ways the room will stay the same.

___ Underline the ways it will be different.

◀ Sample Text Markings

Passage 15: Room and Bored

1 C; *Sample answer:* I picked C because the main idea of the story is to update Kenji's room since he's now older and more mature.

2 A; *Sample answer:* I picked A because I noticed the word *upgrade* in the final paragraph of the story, and it made sense.

3 *Sample answer:* It was babyish before the renovation. With the addition of the new furniture and décor, his room is now better suited to an older boy.

4 *Sample answer:* I think it explores the theme of growing up. Kenji felt out of place in his babyish room now that he was older, so he asked his parents to help it grow with him.

Name _____ Date _____

The Chapman Stick

Read the music story.
Then follow the instructions in the Text-Marking box.

At the music museum, I got to see new and ancient instruments from around the world. They were all quite fascinating. Then I learned that there was going to be a demonstration of a special instrument called a Chapman Stick.

"Good afternoon," said a musician. "Please welcome my band." I was puzzled, because he was by himself. There weren't any other band members on stage beside him. He held something that looked like a guitar, only it didn't have a body. The entire instrument consisted of just a fretboard, which was wider and longer than a guitar's fretboard. It had more strings than a guitar, too.

He plugged the Chapman Stick into an electric amplifier, just like a guitar. Then he began to play. I couldn't believe my ears. I was amazed by all the different sounds the Chapman Stick could make. The instrument sounded like a guitar, a piano, a bass and a drum, all at the same time. I enjoyed hearing the musician play full songs all by himself.

I wish I had a Chapman Stick. I could be a one-boy band. I know what I'm requesting for my birthday this year!

Text Marking

Compare and contrast the Chapman Stick with an electric guitar.

☐ Box signal words for comparing and contrasting.

◯ Circle the ways the instruments are alike.

___ Underline the ways they are different.

◀ Sample Text Markings

Passage 16: The Chapman Stick

1 B; *Sample answer:* I picked B because the museum had new and ancient instruments so I think 'ancient' means very old.

2 C; *Sample answer:* I picked C because the story is told in the first person by someone who is visiting a music museum.

3 *Sample answer:* I think he probably likes music because he is at a music museum and he seems to know enough about music to appreciate learning about a new instrument.

4 *Sample answer:* Both fretboards are the background for the strings of the instrument. Both have tuning pegs at the top and both are long. But the Chapman Stick's fretboard is longer, wider and supports more strings.

Answers

Passage 17: Have You Ever Seen?

1 A; *Sample answer:* I picked A because I think jam is not the fruit flavoured spread that you buy in jars, but the hold-up that happens when there is too much traffic.

2 D; *Sample answer:* I worked out that in this case, the poet was not referring to 'plot' as part of a garden, but the sneaky plan of a complicated story or film.

3 *Sample answer:* I think the poet is pointing out words in English that have different meanings. The poet does this by asking questions that are impossible to answer if you think of the wrong meaning of a word.

4 *Sample answer:* Each line asks a question that makes you think about more than one meaning of a word to determine the meaning that is funny.

◀ **Sample Text Markings**

Passage 18: To Go or Not to Go

1 D; *Sample answer:* I picked D because I think the expression refers to something so unusual, unique and possibly life-changing, it doesn't happen very often.

2 C; *Sample answer:* I picked C because that word is used in paragraph 5, and also, her conversation with Rashid shows that she really wants this adventure.

3 *Sample answer:* Rashid seems like a clever, informed but sceptical person who isn't convinced that this adventure is worth the risks and problems he foresees. On the other hand, his mother, while also clever and informed, seems fearless and more adventurous.

4 *Sample answer:* First of all, it's set in the future – 2048 to be exact. It discusses a possible settlement on Mars, which is not yet possible, though it may happen one day.

SCHOLASTIC

Egg of Chaos

Read the Chinese creation myth.
Then follow the instructions in the Text-Marking box.

At first, the universe was jumbled inside a huge egg. That murky chaos contained all forms of opposites, or *yin* and *yang*. In the whirling mixture were water and fire, night and day, north and south and so on. And there was Pangu, the being who would one day create our world.

Pangu slept inside the egg of chaos for 18,000 years. During that time, the *yin* and *yang* of all things was tangled together. He separated the heavier *yin* from the lighter *yang*. The *yang* floated up to become the sky while the *yin* settled to become the earth.

Standing between the two parts, Pangu's head touched sky and his feet strode upon earth. Over the next 18,000 years, sky and earth grew ever more vast, moving apart by two metres each day.

Pangu also grew, keeping sky and earth separated. By the time of his death, earth and sky had settled into their places. One of Pangu's eyes became the sun, the other the moon. His breath became wind and clouds; his voice turned into the sound of thunder. Pangu's body formed great mountains and his blood its flowing waters. His veins became roads and his muscles fertile fields. His hairs remained in the sky as glittering stars.

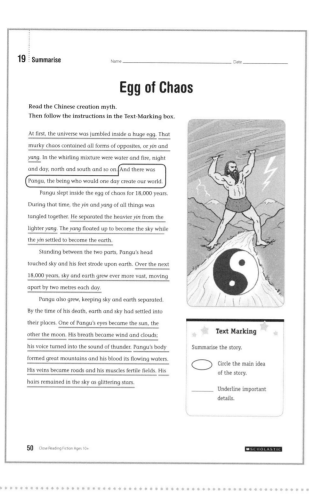

Text Marking

Summarise the story.

◯ Circle the main idea of the story.

___ Underline important details.

Passage 19: Egg of Chaos

1 C; *Sample answer:* I picked C because the author explains this in the second sentence of the piece.

2 B; *Sample answer:* I picked B because in the third and fourth paragraphs, the myth explains the cause of this separation.

3 *Sample answer:* Health and sickness are opposites but related like *yin* and *yang*. Health is being well, while sickness is its opposite – lack of health. One hopes to stay healthy, but sickness can rob one's health at any time.

4 *Sample answer:* The being Pangu grew inside the egg of chaos for 18,000 years, along with all the *yin* and *yang* of the universe. When he broke out of the egg, *yin* and *yang* formed earth and sky. When he died, parts of his body turned into parts of earth and sky.

Febold Feboldson's Find

Read this tall tale from the American Midwest.
Then follow the instructions in the Text-Marking box.

Have you ever seen a popcorn ball? It's a popular American snack, made of popcorn pieces stuck together with syrup and formed into a clump. You might imagine some clever cook thought of this delicious idea. Well, that's NOT how popcorn balls came to exist, at least according to old Febold Feboldson. He claimed that the popcorn ball invented itself during the weird summer of 1874.

Farmers in the American Midwest called that growing season The Year of Striped Weather. That's because it alternated rainy and hot, not day by day, but by sections of cropland. Fields grew in stripes: first you'd see 1.5km-wide stripe of crops wilting in the searing heat, then a 1.5km-wide stripe of waterlogged crops soaking nearly to death.

This was exactly the situation on Febold Feboldson's farm. He grew sweetcorn down in the Dismal River valley and sugar cane up on the hills above. One day the sun baked his sweetcorn plants so much that the kernels popped, causing a yellow blizzard of popcorn. Meanwhile, the rain was drenching his sugar-cane stalks so badly that the syrup inside washed out and flowed down towards the popcorn. A ball soon formed, growing gigantic as it tumbled along. Febold estimated that it was about 60 metres wide!

Febold's neighbour, Bert Bergstrom, witnessed this eye-popping event. Bert offered to help Febold to roll the great popcorn ball into town to impress visitors. But just then, a swarm of hungry grasshoppers devoured the entire very-first popcorn ball.

Text Marking

Summarise the story.
Think about its theme.

◯ Circle the main idea of the story.

___ Underline important details.

Passage 20: Febold Feboldson's Find

1 A; *Sample answer:* I picked A because it is the most sensible answer, based on the story.

2 C; *Sample answer:* I picked C because the other three words are synonyms for being very wet.

3 *Sample answer:* Febold Feboldson's crops grew in such a way that, during the Year of Striped Weather, the popcorn ball invented itself, and he found the first one ever on his farm.

4 *Sample answer:* I think that since this is a tall tale, the whole idea of a popcorn ball inventing itself is nonsense. Then, to have it devoured means there's no proof that it ever existed, and it is just a far-fetched story.

SCHOLASTIC

Available for Lexile Levels BR–1000+

SHORT READS
FICTION AND NON-FICTION

Develop deep comprehension skills with close and repeated reading

✓ Short fiction and non-fiction reading cards for all abilities

✓ Engaging topics and snappy reads across a range of text types

✓ Creative activities for comprehension, peer discussion and writing

✓ Perfect for group reading, pairs or independent reading

✓ Supportive teacher's notes with research-proven techniques

www.scholastic.co.uk/shortreads